ARCHELON

BY KATE MOENING
ILLUSTRATIONS BY MAT EDWARDS

EPIC

BELLWETHER MEDIA • MINNEAPOLIS, MN

EPIC

EPIC BOOKS are no ordinary books. They burst with intense action, high-speed heroics, and shadows of the unknown. Are you ready for an Epic adventure?

Library of Congress Cataloging-in-Publication Data

LC record for Archelon available at: https://lccn.loc.gov/2022050383

Editor: Betsy Rathburn   Designer: Jeffrey Kollock

Printed in the United States of America, North Mankato, MN.

TABLE OF CONTENTS

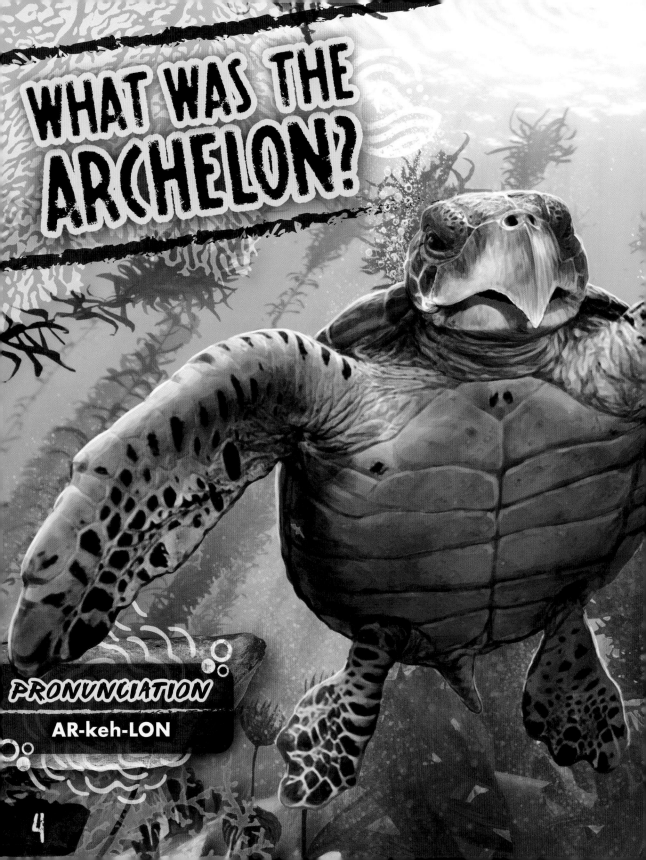

WHAT WAS THE ARCHELON?

Late Cretaceous period

The archelon was a giant sea turtle.
It was the biggest turtle that has ever lived!
It lived about 75 million years ago.
This was in the Late **Cretaceous period**
of the **Mesozoic era**.

The archelon could grow up to 16 feet (4.9 meters) long! It weighed over 4,500 pounds (2,041 kilograms).

shell

flippers

The archelon swam with long **flippers**. Its thin shell helped it float in water.

SIZE COMPARISON

about as long as a car

THE LIFE OF THE ARCHELON

The archelon lived alone. It swam in **shallow** ocean waters. It ate food that floated into its path. Its favorite foods were fish, jellyfish, and **mollusks**. It used its hooked **beak** to crush shells.

beak

ARCHELON DIET

jellyfish

fish

mollusks

The archelon stayed near coasts.
It found more food there.

It **hibernated** on the ocean floor.
It rested under sand and mud for months!

hibernating

The archelon went on land, too.
Females laid eggs on sandy beaches.
They did not take care of their young.
Babies crawled to the ocean on their
own after they **hatched**.

hatching

Mosasaurs and sharks hunted the archelon. Tough **plates** on the archelon's belly kept it safe. Sharp teeth could not break through.

plates

OUT OF THE SHELL

Like today's sea turtles, the archelon could not pull its head or flippers into its shell. Predators often went after these parts first!

sharks

The archelon's size also protected it. Most **predators** did not want to eat such a giant turtle!

FOSSILS AND EXTINCTION

The archelon went **extinct** at the end of the Cretaceous period. This was about 66 million years ago.

Earth's **environment** was changing. The archelon could not survive.

The first archelon **fossil** was found in South Dakota in the 1890s. A large sea once covered this area.

BIG BONES

The largest archelon fossil is named Brigitta. It is displayed in a museum in Austria!

fossil

BIGGEST ARCHELON FOSSIL

UNITED STATES

FOUND in the **1970s**

LOCATED about 45 miles (72 kilometers) south of Rapid City, South Dakota

Scientists have found more archelon fossils nearby. There is still more to learn about this giant turtle!

GET TO KNOW THE ARCHELON

thin shell

LOCATION

ancient oceans in present-day North and South Dakota

WEIGHT

over 4,500 pounds (2,041 kilograms)

FOOD

jellyfish

mollusks

fish

SIZE

up to 16 feet (4.9 meters) long

ERA about 75 million years ago, during the Late Cretaceous period

Paleozoic | Mesozoic | Cenozoic

Cretaceous

hooked beak

long flippers

FIRST FOSSIL FOUND

in the 1890s by G.R. Wieland

21

GLOSSARY

beak—the mouth of an archelon

Cretaceous period—the last period of the Mesozoic era that occurred between 145 million and 66 million years ago; the Late Cretaceous period began around 100 million years ago.

environment—the natural world

extinct—no longer living

flippers—flat body parts that are used for swimming

fossil—the remains of a living thing that lived long ago

hatched—broke out of an egg

hibernated—spent a season sleeping or resting

Mesozoic era—a time in history that happened about 252 million to 66 million years ago; the first birds, mammals, and flowering plants appeared on Earth during the Mesozoic era.

mollusks—animals that have soft bodies and usually have a hard outer shell; some mollusks, such as squids, have an inner shell.

plates—flat, hard pieces that cover the bodies of some animals

predators—animals that hunt other animals for food

shallow—not deep

TO LEARN MORE

AT THE LIBRARY

Sipperley, Keli. *Fossils*. North Mankato, Minn.: Capstone Press, 2021.

Taylor, Charlotte. *Digging Up Sea Creature Fossils*. New York, N.Y.: Enslow Publishing, 2022.

Yang, Yang. *The Secrets of Ancient Sea Monsters: PNSO Encyclopedia for Children*. Dallas, Tex.: Brown Books Kids, 2021.

ON THE WEB

FACTSURFER

Factsurfer.com gives you a safe, fun way to find more information.

1. Go to www.factsurfer.com.

2. Enter "archelon" into the search box and click 🔍.

3. Select your book cover to see a list of related content.

INDEX